The Little Book

For Big

Transformations

31 Days of Inner Visions and Practical Spiritual Practices

2nd Edition

by

Skip Jennings

ISBN: 978-1-913479-18-3 (paperback)
ISBN: 978-1-913479-19-0 (ebook)

That Guy's House
20-22 Wenlock Road
London
England
N1 7GU
www.thatGuysHouse.com

That Guy's House

Dedication

I learned that courage was not the absence of fear, but the triumph over it. The brave man is not he who does not feel afraid, but he who conquers that fear."

~Nelson Mandela

This book is for you, Mom, for always praying for your son.

Bill, your unwavering friendship is a gift to my soul.

Chaune, you are my guiding angel and I miss you every day.

Michael Bernard Beckwith, your wisdom and example continuously inspires me to dive deeper and deeper into my spiritual practices.

Mary Miller, thank you for helping me to discover that writing is a transformative spiritual practice.

My Agape family, thank you for holding the high watch and blessing all beings and the planet one prayer at a time.

Contents

Acknowledgments

It is one of my greatest blessings to have so many inspiring people in my life, and I could not have written this book without the support of their love, encouragement and friendship.

Mom, thank you for being my inspiration from birth. Thank you for being Mom *and* Dad. Your love is everything to me.

Thomas, Cynthia and Chaia, you are the family I chose and I thank you for anchoring me in God. This is our time to shine!

Chaune, you taught me how to be a loving presence on the planet. I am forever blessed and I miss you so much.

Bill Robertson, you inspire me to be a better man and to reach for greatness. I love you my friend.

Reverend Michael Bernard Beckwith, I am grateful to be a part of the Beloved Community of the Agape International Spiritual Center. Thank you for your YES!

Sean Patrick, my deepest appreciation for bringing me into That Guy's House Publishing family of authors.

Karen Mills-Alston, thank you for writing the most inspiring forward for this book.

To the ministers, practitioners, friends and members of Agape—you are my tribe of truth.

Ministers on the rise, we are on a mission, I thank you for the way we lovingly support one another.

To my Agape University facilitators, practitioners, and fellow students, thank you for helping me to discover my innate greatness as an expression of Spirit.

To Rev Susan Shahani and the Enlightened Heart Spiritual Center, I am grateful to be your associate minister. I am blessed, you are blessed, and we are blessed together.

Cyndi Ambriz, thank you for being my teacher, shaman, friend, mentor, business partner. Your light shines so bright as we enter the vortex of samadhi.

Rickie Byars, the songs and music that pour out from your soul inspires me to sing and dance.

Gerrick Angel and the LGBTQA Ministry of Agape, I am blessed to be of service as your co-director.

Rodney Scott, Thank you for your friendship, encouragement and guidance.

To Tom Blumenthal, your friendship and support has been one of the biggest blessings in my life. Thank you!

To my clients, students and fitness family, thank you for creating a space for me to do what I love—it's glorious!

I profoundly thank all of those who have appeared on my life's path.

In divine love and friendship,

Skip

Foreword - A

Have you ever met someone for the first time and intuitively knew that you would be connected for a lifetime? That's how I felt when I met Skip Jennings so it's no surprise that we have continued to weave in-and-out of each other's lives for several years be it in classes at the Agape International Spiritual Center, as Agape Licensed Spiritual Practitioners, or serving together at Agape's annual Revelation Conference.

I know Skip to be a person who is passionately committed to his inward journey. It's simply the way he lives his life—solidly dedicated to his ongoing spiritual evolutionary process, forever saying YES to his inner guidance. Through his calling as an Agape Licensed Spiritual Practitioner and minister on the rise, he enthusiastically reminds us through his writings that "Your birthright is to live a life that is energetic, filled with soulful vitality." I love those words of his because they accurately reflect the energy of his jubilant "amen" and "hallelujah" shout-outs during attendance at Agape services. His joy is contagious as he announces the Allness of existence. What a magnificent way to live!

The Little Book for Big Transformations is a must read as a daily spiritual practice. Skip's writings come from a place of inner brilliance articulated through his unique, courageous voice and when put into practice, allow you to know within that "I am complete and whole, *PERIOD*." Read this book again and again and you will be inspired to wholeheartedly participate—body, mind, and spirit—in this thing called Life.

Karen Mills-Alston, ALSP

Author of *10 Principles for a Life Worth Living*

Foreword - B

Theological and Ministerial Thesis Essay by Skip Jennings

Spiritual transformation is an individual journey that cannot be defined as a systemic methodology and, therefore, requires spiritual practices that are personal and unique to the individual, affecting every aspect of one's life. *The Little Book for Big Transformations* is a spiritual tool for supporting an all-embracing evolution. In writing *The Little Book for Big Transformations*, the author asked three questions: Why is transformation or what Christians identify as salvation only obtained by believing in Jesus? Why is transformation compartmentalized to only a religious experience? Can transformation and spiritual evolution be simple, practical and accessible, initiated by the life experiences one is having at the present moment?

"Transformation is an inside job" is a common adage used by licensed spiritual practitioners and counselors to invite clients to take responsibility for their own evolution. I have has found this to be a foundational principle of truth in my professional practice. Spiritual development requires introspection of one's life, revealing opportunities for growth and creating an upleveling of the current paradigm that affects every aspect of one's life. The spiritual journey cannot be compartmentalized. Transformation is not separate from how we feel or think or how the body operates in the human incarnation. When we choose to embrace the transformational journey as an ongoing way of life, opportunities emerge everywhere. When we are open to belief in the One Mind, another name for God, it is the little "aha" moments that fill us with lessons that ultimately lead to larger transformational awakenings.

The spiritual seeker must recognize that transformation cannot completely occur in a church. To experience a spiritual awakening, we must realize the shift will affect every aspect of our life. For example, when we are in a fitness club participating in a physical practice, driving down a highway, or in a grocery store, there is invariably an opportunity for spiritual growth. True transformation is an ongoing process, and it happens continuously if we are open and willing to evolve. As we grow spiritually, we realize that transformation is as eternal as our souls. Michael Bernard Beckwith teaches the principle that transformation is everlasting. During a Sunday service, he said, "When we transition, we will have more to learn on the other side."

Spiritual lessons are available everywhere if we are open to receive them, and there is an opportunity for growth every moment that we breathe. There are endless evolutionary openings when we agree to live the boundless life we are meant to live. In *The Foundation of Mysticism*, Joel S. Goldsmith explains, "God is present only where God is realized." This is the same for our spiritual journey. The road to enlightenment lies in our willingness to embrace transformation. Something is sacred because it reminds us of the existence of a higher self.

My journey as a personal trainer and fitness coach evolved over 30 years and began with the paradigm that the physical body was separate from the spiritual body. Growing up in the Baptist church, I was accustomed to spiritually-minded people who did not care for their body-temples. They would go to church on Sunday, praise God, sing songs of glory, and receive inspiration from the pastor, then sit down and eat soul food. Fried chicken and collard greens cooked in fatback have nothing to do with the soul, but they tasted like heaven. The cuisine that they ate comforted their emotions, but it was detrimental to their bodies. In their spiritual practice to be good Christians, they strove to follow God's commandments to make it into the pearly gates. However, they missed the opportunity to connect with the Spirit by caring for their bodies created by the Divine. 1 Corinthians 6:19 says, "Do you not know that your bodies are temples of the Holy Spirit, who is in you, whom you have received from God? You are not your own." This verse is not only a question but also a statement inviting us to realize that the body is more than just a body; it is where the spirit of God lives. This is an invitation for us to approach transformation as a holistic methodology. Paul the Apostle invites us to see that we are more than a physical being. He reminds us that the Spirit lives within us and that we belong to God. Michael Beckwith teaches that we are spiritual begins, having a spiritual experience within a human incarnation. 1 Corinthians 10:31 says, "So whether you eat or drink or whatever you do, do it all for the glory of God." This scripture is a mandate for us to care for the body-temple so that we may continue to do God's work. Because our bodies are created by God, there is a directive to care for them. Throughout

The Little Book for Big Transformations, the reader is invited to embrace a physical practice inspired by spirituality. We cannot transform the physical body without embracing and connecting with Spirit that lives within us. In the fitness profession, there has been very little coaching that our bodies are more than physical entities. From gym memberships to streaming fitness services, the transformation of the physical takes a myopic approach. Many spiritual and religious traditions teach that our sacred communities are found primarily within the spaces in which we gather on Sundays. This paradigm creates a very limited view of transformation.

Within the New Thought spiritual tradition, we believe that God is present everywhere and in all things. With this understanding, spiritual transformation is available to us everywhere. To have a *New Thought*, we must be willing to embrace the endless ideas of the spiritual journey. Yet, we can learn from our old religious traditions to create a new paradigm for transformation. If we consider our traditional religious communities as templates for transformation, we can find the same experiences in our fitness clubs. Much like a church, a fitness facility is a place for inspiration, motivation, and transformation to occur. We religiously go to the gym and attend group fitness classes to experience the same vibrational high we experience in our spiritual communities. A group fitness coach, personal trainer, or yoga instructor offers the same inspiration as a minister or pastor. As a fitness coach, my work is to inspire clients and students to transform and live the best life that they are called to live. As a minister, my work is the same. Transformation is not limited to our traditional gatherings. It is present everywhere if we choose. Every person who participates in fitness is seeking something more than just fitting into their skinny jeans whether they are aware of it or not. Fitness enthusiasts set the intention to live their greatest life and to be the best version of themselves. Similarly, as spiritual journeyers, we intend to wake up to the life that we are meant to live. I call this the "cross-bridging" of transformation.

The transformational journey has no limits; there are no separations or barriers except for those that we create. The cross-bridging of transformation exceeds our existing ideas of transformation. Because we are spiritual beings having a spiritual experience in a human incarnation, transformation is not limited to where we gather on a Sunday. *The Little Book for Big Transformations* invites the reader to see that transformation is not in a box, compartmentalized from life structure to life structure or strictly limited to church attendance. Opportunities for transformation are available everywhere. Invitations for spiritual growth can be recognized when one is willing to allow a divine evolution to take place. While a Moses "burning bush" experience or a climb to the top of Mount Everest can lead to self-awareness, most of us do not have those grandiose moments of enlightenment. Transformation comes in many sizes, shapes, and forms at any moment if we are willing; it can take as long as a lifetime, or it can be instantaneous. One is reminded of the lyrics from the Broadway musical *Hello Dolly*'s "It Only Takes a Moment": *"It only, takes a moment, for your eyes to meet, and then...your heart knows, in a moment, you will never be alone again."* This message of how quickly an awaking can happen invites us to see beyond our linear thinking and realize there is no time in God.

Our old cookie-cutter ideas of transformation are limiting. Siddhartha sat underneath the bodhi tree after searching the world for enlightenment, and it was not until he surrendered to the stillness did he awaken as the Buddha. It was with a simple act of defiance that Rosa Parks launched the greatest demonstration of the civil rights movement. Her self-realization led to the decision not to surrender her seat to a white person. Though tired and frustrated, in her moment of awakening, Rosa said enough is enough; that began Alabama's great bus boycott in 1955. Once a slave trader and enslaved person in West Africa, John Newton, on his journey home, experienced a Christian conversion during a storm near the Irish coast in 1778. The next year, he co-wrote "Amazing Grace" with poet William Cowper, which recounts his journey of transformation. For all three, the transformations were unique yet led to shifts that not only altered themselves but also inspired the world to change. *The Little Book for Big Transformations* chronicles my journey of transformation in its many forms with its multiple impacts on me and the communities in which I exist.

As a minister, my calling is to help everyone to see spiritual practices as a way of life. This pathway to enlightenment is not about finding God; God does not need to be found. This spiritual experience is about understanding where we land in the omnipresence of God. My message is achievable and practical transformation. It requires growth work, but it does not need to be hard or airy-fairy. It is functional — applied and initiated from one's everyday life.

Transformation is defined as a dramatic change in form or appearance. Synonyms in Webster's dictionary are *alteration, modification, variation, conversion, and revision.* During the journey of awakening, all these words are applicable. There is an *alteration* in the mind and body when we set the intention to align our human incarnation with the perfection of the Spirit. There is a *modification* in our paradigm and how we think as we become aware of the spiritual laws that govern our lives and begin to use them. This is when we align our thinking with the One Mind. As the foundation of spiritual transformation, the greatest law says, "It is done as we believe." The shift begins with our thinking. A *variation* in our experience of God is inevitable We begin to experience the presence of God more deeply and profoundly. There is a *conversion* in our belief system allowing us to identify what we truly believe, as opposed to beliefs that were handed down to us from previous generations. A *revision* of our daily spiritual practices takes place because we have outgrown our old paradigms. The way these transformations take shape is purely designed by an individual willingness to transform.

The Little Book for Big Transformations supports the philosophy that transformation cannot be explained or qualified as a purely religious experience. Enlightenment is a personal experience that transcends traditional religious teachings. Everyday experiences of transformation are revealed through the personal essays identifying the omniactivity of God. Sharing stories of feeling stuck and alone, or remembering the loving home that my mother created, or coming out as a gay man invites the reader to connect through common life experiences, ultimately revealing my personal transformation. *The Little Book for Big Transformations* recounts this journey, and the opportunity a shift emerges in infinite ways. Transformation is simple and accessible when we remain mindful and willing. I intend for the reader to recognize daily opportunities for spiritual growth. Awakening can happen in a brief moment, but it can also be a lifelong journey with no ETA. As I shares my struggles and triumphs as a minster, I intends to be transparent and approachable. I want readers to see my everyday experiences as familiar. We have all experienced loss, heartbreak, and the desire to overcome addiction and physical disease. The circumstances may be different, but the intention is the same — spiritual liberation and transformation.

I present personal transformation as a four-step process: inspiration to change, challenges, awakening, and practical applications to solidify change. *The Little Book for Big Transformations* is a 31-day devotional tool that contains a four-step theme in every essay. Step 1: Inspiration: The essays open with inspirational quotes from spiritual teachers. Step 2: Challenges: Subjects or challenges that require insight and provide opportunities for growth are presented. Step 3: Awakening: I share personal "aha moments" and the transformation that has taken place. Step 4: Application: Affirmations to empower transformation are explored.

When ministers share personal challenges and awakenings as tools in teaching. Many have found *The Little Book for Big Transformations* uplifting, authentic, and transformational. When ministers find the freedom to talk about the ups and downs of their spiritual journeys, they become accessible and trustworthy, creating the realization that we are all the same.

"This book is a priceless gift to all those yearning to live a richer, more purposeful and creative life," says Michael Beckwith. I intend to inspire people to find a practice that resonates with them. *The Little Book for Big Transformations* is a spiritual tool that supports the message that transformation is practical for and accessible to all, transformation and salvation is not only obtained by believing in Jesus and awakening is not compartmentalized to only a religious experience. Spiritual evolution can be simple, practical and accessible, initiated by the life experiences in the present moment?

The Analysis

Based on *The Little Book for Big Transformations* as it Applies to Ministry

I present personal transformation as a four-step process: inspiration to change, challenges, awakening, and practical applications to solidify change. *The Little Book for Big Transformations* is a 31-day devotional tool that contains a four-step theme in every essay. Step 1: Inspiration: The essays open with inspirational quotes from spiritual teachers. Step 2: Challenges: Subjects or challenges that require insight and provide opportunities for growth are presented. Step 3: Awakening: I share personal "aha moments" and the transformation that has taken place. Step 4: Application: Affirmations to empower transformation are explored.

When ministers share personal challenges and awakenings as tools in teaching. Many have found *The Little Book for Big Transformations* uplifting, authentic, and transformational. When ministers find the freedom to talk about the ups and downs of their spiritual journeys, they become accessible and trustworthy, creating the realization that we are all the same. *The Little Book for Big Transformations* reflects my personal journey of awakening. Because transformation is a spiritual evolution, *The Little Book for Big Transformations* chronical three chapters in my life which I have named *The Seeker, The Grower* and *The Teacher*. The early entries in the book talks about my search for a God that lives within me. The middle potion is an account of deep spiritual development. The last section is about becoming a spiritual teacher and leader. Through my writings I can recognize the growth that has taken place during the past 10 years. I have observed this three-phase transformation in many of my clients and *The Little Book for Big Transformations* is an invitation to my readers to recognize their own evolution as it is taking place.

I intend to inspire people to find a practice that resonates with them. *The Little Book for Big Transformations* is a spiritual tool that supports the message that transformation is practical for and accessible to all, the experience of transformation and salvation is not only obtained by believing in Jesus and awakening is not compartmentalized to only a religious experience. Spiritual evolution can be simple, practical and accessible, initiated by the life experiences in the present moment?

INTRODUCTION

Transformation and The Big Yes

—————— ◇◇ ——————

"Take the first step in faith. You don't have to see the whole staircase, just take the first step."
~Dr. Martin Luther King

"We are spiritual beings, having a human incarnation."
~Michael Bernard Beckwith

It was approximately two years after the first episode of *The Oprah Winfrey Show* in September of 1986 that I heard Oprah use the term "Aha moments." I instantly related to it, because it described those pivotal moments which propelled me from my Southern Baptist upbringing to Mormonism Then onto the Episcopal Church where I was close to becoming a priest. Ultimately, I landed at the doorstep of the New Thought movement where I found my spiritual tribe. Today, whenever I'm asked to state my religious affiliation my reply is "I am a Universalist" because applying another Oprahism, if there's *"one thing I know for sure"* it is this: That which we call God transcends all religions.

No matter what path resonates with one's spirit all spiritual traditions have their origin in *Divine Love*. As the master teacher Jesus the Christ teaches in Mark 12:30-31: *"The first of all the commandments is thou shalt love the Lord thy God with all thy heart...and the second is this, thou shalt love thy neighbor as thyself."* In his "Four Elements of True Love," the Buddha taught that loving-kindness (*maitri*) is the desire to offer happiness to others; compassion (*karuna*) is the desire to remove suffering from others; joy *(mudita)* is the desire to bring joy to people around you; and equanimity (*upeksha*) is the desire to not discriminate. In Islam, Muslims are directed by Allah (God) in the ways of connecting with him through acts of love, for as the prophet Muhammad teaches, "Feed the hungry and visit a sick person. Free the captive if he be unjustly confined and assist any person oppressed whether Muslim or non-Muslim." In the Hindu scripture the *Mahabharata*, Lord Krishna stated, "But of all the qualities I could name, verily love is the highest."

One of my most tangible experiences of Spirit's love took place in 2005, during a meditation session at the Agape International Spiritual Center, I was inwardly enveloped in such a blissful embrace of Divine Love I began to uncontrollably weep tears of indescribable joy. The weight of years of self-condemnation was lifted from my heart as this Love dissolved the false belief that I would be condemned to an eternity in hell for my identity as a gay man and for whom I choose to love.

2

This compassionate, tender, unconditional love of Spirit is unceasingly poured out to us all.

Throughout my early years in school, I received poor grades in reading, writing, and arithmetic. Although this was more than compensated through my gifts in the creative arts, I still questioned why those other subjects were so challenging for me, until it was discovered that I had experienced severe dyslexia. It then became my intention to move beyond my self-assigned labels of being stupid and illiterate by writing and publishing a book. Which I did. *Spirit Explosion: A Time for God, Love and Transformation* allowed me to drop the false labels I had ascribed to myself for far too many years. Because writing had become a source of healing for me, my prayer was that my book would inspire its readers to also use writing as a healing, transformative tool, whether it was in the form of a personal journal or a book.

In 2010, I graduated from Agape University's Practitioner Studies program and was invited to contribute to its *Inner Visions Magazine*, a monthly publication written by licensed spiritual practitioners and ministers. After receiving positive feedback from my first submission, I began contributing regularly. Not only did my submissions support me spiritually, they gave me the courage to co-write a second book, *The Lotus Kitchen*, a vegetarian cookbook which includes yoga practices.

This book you hold in your hands combines 31 submissions I made to Agape's *Inner Visions* magazine. They have been freshly edited since their original publication dates for the purpose of reflecting my ever-evolving spiritual odyssey, my hero's journey home to my Divine Self. My prayer is that each day's reading will ignite a flame in your own heart to live the life to which your soul is calling you.

DAY 1

Stuck No More

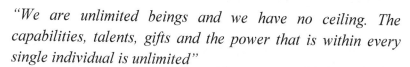

"We are unlimited beings and we have no ceiling. The capabilities, talents, gifts and the power that is within every single individual is unlimited"

~Michael Bernard Beckwith

Taken from the wisdom teachings of Michael Bernard Beckwith, founder of the Agape International Spiritual Center, the quote above is one of my favorites. How grateful I am to know that "every moment" includes even those when our inner growth appears to have gone into hibernation, into what I have come to call a time of *"sacred gestation"* during which we are being prepared to step into our next evolutionary leap. Our willingness to enter this intimate tryst with our Higher Self moves us in the direction we are being guided to both embrace and release on our journey to self-realization.

The depth of our commitment to our inner growth sets in motion a clearing out of outgrown beliefs, opinions, conditioning, and patterns of behavior which no longer serve us.

At this juncture it is vital to ask two questions: What qualities am I being called *to cultivate*, and what must I *release* for aligning with Spirit's vision for the next stage of my spiritual growth?

Another skillful evolutionary tool, no matter how long you've been on your spiritual path is the practice of what Suzuki Roshi calls "the beginner's mind." The beginners mind keeps you open, receptive, and teachable, freeing yourself for past experiences that can affect the present. You may want to use the "set aside prayer": *"I set aside everything I think I know about _____ (fill in the blank) so that I may have a new experience."* Be willing to release everything that no longer serves, creating a space for transformation and new ideas to be birthed. Now state with authority, "I AM STUCK NO MORE!"

Affirmation: Today, I am willing to have a new experience in God. My life is filled with infinite divine ideas. My consciousness is an expanded expression of the One. I am the Universe in the flesh, therefore I am stuck no more. And so, it is.

DAY 2

Life After Life

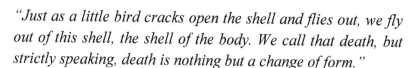

"Just as a little bird cracks open the shell and flies out, we fly out of this shell, the shell of the body. We call that death, but strictly speaking, death is nothing but a change of form."

~**Swami Satchitananda**

In 2012, I experienced a profound sense of loss when my sister, Beth, two aunts, several close family friends and a student of mine all transitioned into their new dimension of living. There were days when I felt as though my life had lost its buoyancy and joy without the physical presence of these dear ones. Turning to my spiritual counselor for some words of wisdom, I was comforted by her suggestion that I practice a contemplative meditation on the impermanence of life on planet Earth, and the permanence of the Eternal Life of the individual soul. In my meditations I asked the Universe to grace me with an understanding of the principle of eternality. When I did so, I felt the precious presence of my beloved ones surrounding me. Eventually, I realized it was my own fears around death and dying that were at the root of my experience of loss.

Yoga master B.K.S. Iyengar once said, *"The most*

important pose during a yoga session is Shavasana." Some yoga teachers refer to it as the *"corpse pose,"* because it's done lying flat on one's back, eyes closed, with arms extended to one's side in a position of complete repose, mindfully reminding us of that existential moment when we will exhale our last breath and transition to the invisible side of life. Adding meditation, yoga, mantras, affirmations, and spiritual study to your spiritual toolkit will contribute to preparing you to skillfully work with your relationship to death, to make friends with it as you move from lifetime to lifetime.

Today, remember you are created by the Universe and you are eternal. Set the intention to know your *Infinite-self*; it is our spiritual practice which allows us to tap into a place of peace. Close your eyes, take a breath and contemplate *life eternal*. Be still and know that your spirit can never die.

Affirmation: Today, I live the eternal life of God with high intentions. My life is the blessing that anchors heaven throughout the world and all is well. I am the light of love, everlasting. And so it is. Amen.

DAY 3

We Are Nature

"You carry Mother Earth within you. She is not outside of you."

~Thich Nhat Hanh

We know only one planet as our human home, It isn't called Mother Earth for no reason, for she mothers us as her very own children. We carry her within us in the form of the nourishment she provides through her resources of water, food, air, sunshine, and rain. Sadly, however, it seems humanity is overlooking its responsibility to reciprocate by taking loving, grateful care of our Mother. The challenges of water shortage, the extinction of animals and plants, climate change—to name a few, are man-made and can be eliminated through humanity's united commitment and efforts.

It's time to begin acknowledging our oneness with Mother Earth and asking ourselves if there are ways in which we are knowingly or unknowingly contributing to her desecration and instead become agents for her healing and restoration. For example: Can we collectively stop generating more landfills through recycling and composting? Can we plant trees, grow organic vegetables without using pesticides that desecrate the soil? Can we begin this shift today and leave a legacy to our children that include learning how to be caretakers of our earthly home?

I offer this mindful action plan, and should you choose to practice it, for 30 days contemplate and journal the ways in which you can personally contribute to protecting Mother Earth. Pledge your willingness to become part of the solution, for as Mahatma Gandhi reminds us, *"Be the change you want to see."* Remember, we are not just one with nature; we are nature itself, so we must take care of our Mother, ourselves and all beings with whom we share our Earth home.

Affirmation: Today, I choose to care for our precious Mother Earth. I am the blessing that heals this planet, a universal energy that brings forth new ideas. I am the solution! I am the healer! And so I am. Amen.

Renewing the Mind, Body and Spirit

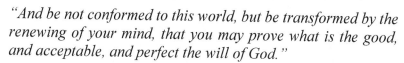

"And be not conformed to this world, but be transformed by the renewing of your mind, that you may prove what is the good, and acceptable, and perfect the will of God."

~Romans 12:2

Many of my "Aha" moments are downloaded during my daily workouts, which I have come to call *"physical spiritual practice."* For example, there are times when a run clears my mind, allowing me to enter a receptive mode and begin catching inner guidance about various facets of my life. The physical practice is a conduit for new ideas to flow and for contemplation to take place within my soul. Those who dance the tango, a vigorous dance of surrender have compared its energy to meditation. The practice of yoga is a form of mental focus, experiencing our capability to improve physical flexibility. Movement cross trains body, mind and spirit, creating a whole-person immersion in the Self.

A good cardio workout focuses our attention on our breath, reminding us that the breath connects us to the soul. Strength training anchors a strong connection to Spirit. Yoga postures remind us not only to be flexible in our body, but in all aspects of our lives. Physical movement enlivens and rejuvenates us and the more we relate to it as a spiritual practice we will become encouraged to include it in our daily routine. Caring for our body temple as the vehicle of our soul represents a deep bow of gratitude to Spirit for the miracle the body is.

I welcome you to consider how you can connect movement to your spiritual practice by inviting yourself to consciously notice if there are "Aha" moments that occur during your exercise routine that you simply haven't yet recognized. It is our thoughts which separate us from the awareness of God so build your mental strength. The physical practice helps us to restore and heal the temple of the Holy Spirit. Today, as we train the body we empower the mind and we unleash our greatness. Set the intention to connect with God fully, mind body and spirit.

Affirmation: Today, I renew my mind, body, and spirit with the Love of God and movement. I infuse love, during my daily practice. I am blessed and a blessing. And so it is.

Divine Independence

———————— ◇ ————————

"I release and I let go, I let the Spirit run my life."
~Song lyric by Rickie Byars and Michael Bernard
Beckwith

"*I release and I let go, I let the Spirit run my life*" is a lyric from my favorite song that sing at the Agape International Spiritual Center. I love its invitation to identify and release patterns of thoughts, beliefs, behaviors, and relationships which substitute for the fulfillment only communion with the Higher Self can provide. For example, when was the last time you asked yourself: *"How can I free myself from the thoughts, beliefs, actions, people and things that no longer serve me?" "Do I use food, drugs, alcohol, sex, work, shopping or social media to fill the empty spaces within myself, and if so, how may I break free from their grip?"*

The good news is the Essential Self can never be enslaved, hurt, harmed, or demolished. However, until we learn to live in the *"let-go,"* the human self can become derailed from discovering and living life centered in Spirit. Although, Spirit is absolute it won't interfere with our choices. When we invite its guidance and grace into our lives with a willingness to accept and apply it, we integrate the human and divine aspects of our being.

When we are willing to release our attachment to that which no longer serves our spiritual evolutionary growth a new world opens up, one of freedom that comes from living in the *"let-go."* Today celebrate the freedom of your soul. Release and turn everything over to God. So when you find yourself biting the hook of habit, burst into singing the lyric, *"I release and I let go, I let the Spirit run my life,"* and watch what happens!

Affirmation: Today, I release and I let Go. I am worthy of true freedom. God is my life. I am a strong pillar of *Divine Independence* rooted in Grace. I am here for God. And so it is. Amen

DAY 6

Love: The Calling

"Love is what we are in our essence, and the more love we feel in our hearts the more it will be brought to us."

~Deepak Chopra

On June 12, 2016, a gunman killed 49 people and injured 53 others in The Pulse, a gay nightclub in Orlando, Florida. As a gay man, I experienced a myriad of emotions that swung from sadness to anger to compassion to love. A few days later, while participating at Agape's LGBTQA healing circle I realized I was still holding on to the hurt and anger out of the fear of forgetting, how such a tragedy affects all those who experience it. Then, while in meditation some days later, I felt guided to lean into the energy of love, When I did, my previous feeling of anger was transformed into that of love and compassion.

Love is the highest consciousnesses from which we can choose to live and move. Under any and all conditions love is the winning argument, the ultimate healer. The power of love is unstoppable and is as healing medicine. When *Love* is used as a

15

tool for healing, we anchor ourselves in God. We are *Love* therefore we can love in any situation.

Today, whenever I learn about another mass shooting my first response is to immediately go into prayer for all concerned, the victims *and* perpetrators. Each of us is a transmitter of energy, and the vibration of prayer travels through the ethers reaching, touching, blessing and healing all those for whom we pray. We are, all of us, potential beacons of light who can shine love into the dark spaces. Whenever tragedy erupts through human actions we must lean into love as the most powerful antidote for humanity's inhumanity to man.

Affirmations: Today, I lean into the power of Love. I am a unique expression of God, exceptional and beautiful. My life is a vehicle for sharing Joy in every situation. I am here to bring the Christ Consciousness into this dimension and I anchor heaven on earth. And so it is. Amen.

Be Still and Return to God

"Return and know that I AM GOD. I am exalted among the nations and I am exalted in the Earth."

~Psalms 46:10

I love when summer arrives because it gives me permission to slow down, relax, and take it easy. The collective energy of the season is about vacation, beach outings, outdoor concerts and social events with our loved ones. Then, when summer comes to an end, the challenge is how to maintain a state of *"sacred relaxation."* The good news is that seasonal shifts do not have to throw us off course. We can return, again and again to an inner state of relaxation by bringing our awareness back to the "now" moment.

When I find myself getting caught up in everyday distractions I turn to yoga as my year-round practice for slowing down and reentering to the present moment. Yoga asanas, also known as the "stillness" or "the seat," require us to stop and reconnect to the Higher Self residing in the tranquility of the soul. As the Yoga Sutra of Patanjali 1:3 teaches, *"Tada drashtuh svarupe vasthanam: then the seer abides in itself, in its true nature, also known as self-realization."*

As a teacher of yoga, it is clear to me the practice represents the allegorical battle between the soul and the ego. Our soul's desire is to live from the divine-self, while the ego's nature is a mindset of me, myself, and I. *The Bhagavad Gita,* sacred scriptures for the yoga practice, say, *"When thy mind, that may be wavering in the contradictions of many scriptures, shall rest unshaken in divine contemplation, then the goal of Yoga is thine."* In other words, if we can allow our thoughts to fall into God, we will know Oneness. God wants to have a sacred encounter with us on a daily basis. It is prayer and meditation which helps us to know our true nature. When we choose the path of stillness we will know the power that sustains us. Today, remember to be still and know that God is God.

Affirmation: Today, I remember to be still and know that God is everything. God is revealed as me. From the stillness I move in a mighty way. And so it is. Amen

DAY 8

Fulfilling the Dreams within You

"The biggest adventure you can take is to live the life of your dreams."

~Oprah Winfrey

"I am able to do all things through the one who strengthens me."

~Philippians 4:13

D o you ever find yourself inwardly saying, "Sure, I'll do that someday, like when… (fill in the blank)? It's no wonder one of the greatest obstructions to fulfilling our intention to live our dreams is procrastination, a trickster that constructs logical arguments, rationalizations, justifications—in plain language: excuses. Try as we may, we can't circle *"someday"* on the calendar, and as is commonly pointed out, *"Tomorrow isn't a day of the week."*

We are here to fulfill our heart's deepest dreams and implanted within us by our Creator Source is all we require for doing so. Let the waiting, procrastinating, excuse-making game stop today! Move in rhythm with the mantra *"It is already done"*—not just in your imagination, but as a reality you are equipped to manifest in the three-dimensional world.

You are Spirit's masterpiece, its divine idea in the flesh. The Universe loves you so much that it created you from the very fabric of itself. The power to fulfill your dreams is the God-seed implanted within your *DNA: Divine Natural Authenticity.* The seeds of love, creativity, joy, abundance, intuition and wisdom are seeking to bloom within you. Will you spend time in meditation today and fertilize these sacred seeds so that they may blossom into flowers of fulfillment?

Affirmation: Today, I have everything that I need. I can do all things and I am empowered with Divine authority. I am the God quality unleashed in its fullness. And so it is.

From Story To Solution

"Prayer is the medium of miracles; in whatever way works for you, pray right now."

~**Marianne Williamson**

Before I learned the metaphysical principles taught in the New Thought tradition of spirituality, I believed God had a distribution problem when it came to blessings. I had the notion that certain people were receivers of blessing and favor, while others were somehow undeserving. Coming from a Baptist upbringing, I thought the blessing of answered prayer was a reward for God-fearing meritorious behavior. Yup, that was my story about not being included in the roll call of the worthy ones. At last, when I began attending Agape and embracing the practice of affirmative prayer, I soon realized that Spirit does not discriminate when it comes to blessings. The Universe does not know whether or not we act appropriately. Our prayers manifest from consciousness. The scripture says, *"It is done as you believe."*

If we pray from a place of fear, fear is the energy we manifest. The Universe reacts to the vibrations and emotions, not the words we speak. We must be mindful, not only what we pray for but also where we *pray from*.

Find the spiritual quality that is seeking to emerge from your situation. If we pray for money, connect with the quality of abundance. If we are dealing with relationship issues, remember self-love. If we are faced with health challenges, connect with divine wholeness. Ask yourself, *what divine quality is seeking to emerge*. Write out your prayers and make a list of any insights revealed to you. The situation is just a story with limited power. Release your story and embrace the glory.

Affirmation: Today, I pray from a consciousness that I am a cup filled with Spirit's blessings, pressed down and overflowing in all aspects of my life.

DAY 10

Election Day Blues? Bring the Light!

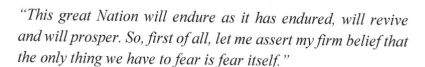

"This great Nation will endure as it has endured, will revive and will prosper. So, first of all, let me assert my firm belief that the only thing we have to fear is fear itself."

~Franklin D. Roosevelt

For two days before the 2016 presidential election I found myself drenched in perspiration as I fearfully awaited its outcome. While in meditation, I became aware that fear had become more prominent in my consciousness than faith. In that moment of awareness, I returned to what I truly believed, that the Light is more powerful than darkness. I began to remember that God is omnipresent, omnipotent, and omniscient, and that its laws governing the universe prevail. I also reminded myself that as a nation we were in a time of a major transformation. Lyrics from Carole King's song, *"I Feel the Earth Move,"* matched my state of mind: *"I feel the earth move under my feet / I feel the sky tumblin' down / I feel my heart start to tremblin'."* Two days later, I could swear I felt the earth have a seismic shakeup. After all, my chosen candidate did not win the electoral vote and all I could say was *#Heartbroken!*

One week after the election, I had a *"this is what I know for sure"* moment: No matter what the outcome, this election has the potential to be a catalyst for unity, even if it looks like we're approaching it walking backwards. This election brought to light all we have not been willing to address that divides us as a human family including racism, sexism, homophobia, misogyny, greed—all of which is telling us its time for a skillful, compassionate global conversation. When healing is required, whether on a collective or a personal level, it is by bringing in the Light that the darkness will be dispelled. When alchemy takes place, there is always a small amount of gold present within the metal. So, if you're experiencing post-election-day blues bring in the Light and know that everything is in divine order according to the laws governing the Universe.

Affirmation: Today, I walk in peace, trusting fully in Spirit's laws governing the universe.

DAY 11

Ignite Your Transformation

"Don't you realize that your body is the temple of the Holy Spirit, who lives in you and was given to you by God? You do not belong to yourself."

~1 Corinthians 6:19

"Do not allow yesterday's garbage to influence your experience today. It is unnecessary to punish yourself for being human."

~Iyanla Vanzant

I t all begins with an intention, which then takes the form of a goal. Our intentions and goals reflect what we believe is possible for us to accomplish in our lives. No matter how many times we may become distracted or stray from them we can press the restart button again, again, and again. This willingness to begin again is fueled by our intentions. There's no need to become discouraged or give up on ourselves, because within all of us is everything we need to reach our goals. Each day is a new day. We have the choice to review, renew and reinvigorate our intentions. They relate to the healthy maintenance of our body and the spiritual evolutionary progress of our mind and spirit.

According to the metaphysical translation of the Bible, the word heaven means *"expansive good."* So what do you say, why not put your intentions and goals into action and let them be a gateway to living in heaven on Earth? Like the iconic brand Nike urges us, *"Just do it!"* Let your intention be the connective tissue that joins together body, mind, and spirit. Become motivated to strengthen the body by walking, dancing, or whatever form of exercise your level of health allows. Nourish the mind with inspiration that expands your knowledge and understanding. Connect with your spirit through meditation, affirmative prayer, and spiritual study. Keep before you the truth that your body is the temple of God, your mind is its creative channel and your spirit is a cathedral where you live in communion with the Divine. Remember, intention creates the reality of our everyday experiences.

Affirmation: Today, I am one in God and I push the divine restart button to ignite the journey of transformation. I live in the newness of every moment. I boldly step into a "just do it" mindset and thrive in the Spirit.

DAY 12

House of Love

"And remember, as it was written, to love another person is to see the face of God."

~Les Misérables

"While we may love each other and never stop loving each other, so often we stop 'showing' each other love."

~Lisa Nichols

When you enter your house, do you feel welcomed into a dominant energy-field of love? Ideally, our house evolves into a home, a sanctuary of love that elevates and enriches our heart and spirit. It is also felt by those who enter its doors.

Growing up in Atlantic City, New Jersey, I distinctly remember how my mother was always there to greet me with a loving smile and a snack when I arrived home from school each day. She would ask me about my day, what I had done and how it went. Truly, she was the *"love activator"* for my brother and me, eager to hear from us and respond, *"Good job!"* Her interest and appreciation for what we reported to her filled our home with an amazing love-energy. As an adult looking back upon those precious years, I can see that my Mom set a clear intention to have our house be a home where she shared her love as a way of encouraging and inspiring us.

I invite you to take on the role of being a *"Love Activator"* and establish a vibrant atmosphere of love in your home. Perhaps you could begin by doing a house blessing, including every room. It is also helpful to bring to mind times when love prevailed in your life. Then, in a stream of consciousness record it in your journal, write a poem, or record in some way your memories of showing up for life in a state of love. Read your writings out loud to yourself or someone close to you. As you feel the words you're reading, bask in their vibration. Soak them in and remember you are a member of the family of God, filled with limitless opportunities to love.

Affirmation: Today, I create a house of Love everywhere I go. My life is a living breathing home for the Universe to have its way. And so it is. Amen.

DAY 13

The Study of Me

"To know thyself is the beginning of wisdom."

~**Socrates**

To know yourself as the Being underneath the thinker, the stillness underneath the mental noise, the love and joy underneath the pain, is freedom, salvation, enlightenment.

~**Eckhart Tolle**

For the past 20 years, the crown jewel of my practice has been taking spiritual classes and independently studying the writings of respected awakened masters and teachers. Every time I sit with my fellow students in the presence of a genuine teacher, "Aha" moments become amplified. I am amazed at the insights I receive from my classmates as well as from students in the classes I have the blessing of facilitating. I journeyed through ministerial studies, my love and appreciation for spiritual education continuously grew. Perhaps the most profound teaching for me has been the realization that spiritual education is a deeper and deeper discovery of who and what I really am. As Suzuki Roshi reminds us, *"In the beginner's mind there are many possibilities, but in the expert's mind there are few."*

Our ultimate assignment during our human incarnation is to become intimately, directly acquainted with the *True Self*. The great philosopher Socrates called it *"laughable"* to endeavor to attain knowledge about deep subjects without first knowing oneself. It was by setting an intention to know myself that I realized his mandate to "know thyself" was even possible! Our quest for awakening is the inner impulse residing in our soul's *DNA: Divine, Natural, Authenticity*. Once we have tasted an appetizer of what that means, we can't live without the *entrée* of self-realization. No matter how we distract ourselves, whether it's social media, eating or shopping there is a Great Something that pulls us back to our spiritual studies and practices. The sleeping giant has woken up and we are left with no choice but to feed it.

Today, set an intention to go within and activate your divine genetic code through meditation, prayer or study. Place notes where you can see them—on your refrigerator, phone, or desk—and let them remind you that you are a spiritual being having a human incarnation.

Affirmation: Today, I embrace the fire of spiritual study and put into practice what I have learned. My divine vibrational frequency is on and *Divine Knowing* is my birthright. Amen.

Your Inner GPS

"Intuition is a spiritual faculty and does not explain, but simply points the way."

~Florence Scovel Shinn

To whom do you listen, the daily news, family, friends, or authority figures? Is your journey guided by societal or cultural opinions, beliefs, or collective thoughts of the status quo? Or, are you tuning into your inner *GPS, God Positioning System*, the intuitive intelligence of your heart-soul? This is the voice of clarity that will let you know when you are on the right track or if a different route is required. The outer world will tell you the sky is falling; God will tell you the sky is the limit!

Certainly, there are ups and downs on the road of life, however, we can change lanes or turn the corner immediately upon receiving intuitive guidance from Spirit. No doubt there are many times when you have said, *"Something just told me to..."* What is that *"something?"* It is your consciousness waking up to the voice of God within you, listening to it, which leads to following it. Sometimes, at first, we don't trust that inner voice. We question it until it becomes so consistent and proves itself right so many times we can no longer ignore it. We learn to trust it, cherish it, and be grateful for it.

We've grown up listening to the adage, *"Listen to your head and not your heart,"* but that's only the ego trying to protect itself. Instead, practice the opposite and listen to the heart's guidance, because it is a very wise, intuitive organ that speaks directly from Spirit.

Affirmation: Today, my inner *GPS* is on and attuned to Spirit. I listen, trust, and surrender to its inner voice as it guides every step of my day.

DAY 15

The Love Practice

"We need joy as we need air. We need Love as we need water. We need each other as we need the earth we share."

~ **Maya Angelou**

"You must have a daily practice. It is our practice that brings us into a place of authentic alignment."

~ **Rev Arlene Cecelia Hylton**

It has been, said by spiritual teachers across all traditions that the purpose of our human incarnation is to discover and rediscover that we are individualized expressions of God. When we give our unconditional "Yes" to this divine mission, we dive deeper into the realization of our purpose to be a beneficial presence on the planet. As Mahatma Gandhi reminds us, *"Be the change you want to see."* The key word in his statement is *"be"*—which is a call to action. For example, we can tell ourselves we want to be more loving, but until we are challenged to love a difficult person, can we say we are *"being"* love?

For me personally, the challenge to my Love Practice is around President 45. In one spiritual community in which I participate one of the main teachings is the practice of *"principles before personalities."* When my ability to love becomes challenged I know I'm being called to put my Love Practice into action. I do this by reminding myself that Divine Love flows in and through my heart restoring me to the truth that Love is the ultimate healer.

Today, I extend to you an invitation to embrace the Love Practice, especially in challenging situations and toward seemingly unlovable individuals. Be a fierce Love Warrior! Whatever daily practice supports you in loving, whether it's meditation, prayer, yoga, or being of service, stand strong in its Light. Stay awake in Love. The call is clear—will you answer it?

Affirmation: Knowing that the unconditional love of God is the very fabric of my being, I freely and unconditionally apply it in all situations and extend it to all those who cross my path.

Remembering Who I AM

"Mother Nature indeed had a glorious birth. Mankind is a child of the Sun."

~ Song Lyrics by Dr. Rickie Byars and Rev Michael Bernard Beckwith

How wondrous it is to know that we are children of the creative Source of the cosmos. Having been made in its image, the power to co-create our lives has been implanted in our innermost essence. The practices of meditation and affirmative prayer activate these co-creative capacities, empowering us to express our highest potential in all aspects of our lives.

The essence of this Power and Presence is revealed in its fullness when we are centered within in a state of genuine stillness. As the teacher and mystic Dr. Howard Thurman tells us, *"We will only know how to use this power by entering into the 'upper room' that lives within our soul."* The Psalmist also wisely encourages us to *"Be still and know that I am God."* It is during our moments of inner stillness that we can hear our soul cry out, *"You are whole, perfect, and complete."* When we hear this cry well up from deep within, we begin to remember the *I AM* consciousness that we are.

Today, embody the truth that the *I AM* of your soul can never be hurt, harmed, or endangered. There is no situation; circumstance or condition that can destroy our Essential Essence, for the *I AM* is indestructible. When the sea of life is raging around you, listen to the still small voice within reminding you of the words of the master teacher Jesus the Christ, *"Peace, be still,"* words he spoke from a state of inner authority, the same inner authority that resides within your I AM consciousness.

Affirmation: Today, I am a child of the sun. I speak from the I AM consciousness and proclaim, *"Peace, be still."*

Perfect Order

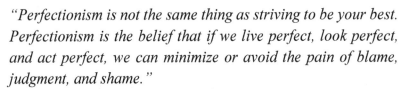

"Perfectionism is not the same thing as striving to be your best. Perfectionism is the belief that if we live perfect, look perfect, and act perfect, we can minimize or avoid the pain of blame, judgment, and shame."

~Brene Brown

My name is Skip and I am a self-proclaimed recovering perfectionist. The first step for recovery is admitting there is a problem. From a young age, I knew I had perfectionism issues. My clothes had to always match. Even if I did not have it all together, I wanted to appear to others that I did. Many years later, when I graduated from NYU with honors, my GPA was just under a 4.0 below the bar of excellence I held up for myself. Hard-wired to strive for perfection, I desired to live a pristine life, even successfully hiding an addiction to cocaine. As my insides where falling apart, I strove mightily to make the outside appear to be perfect.

Fast-forward a magnificent gift fell into my life—Brene Brown's book, *The Gift of Imperfection*. It was then I realized how every aspect of my life, inwardly and outwardly, was run by the myth of perfection to avoid dealing with the shame of what I believed defined *"failure."* Today, I am content with my imperfectly perfect self because I recognize every seeming misstep was—and continues to be—a stepping-stone to my Authentic Self. As a personal trainer, I emphasize to my clients that going to the gym isn't to push ourselves beyond yesterday's endurance, but to show love, caring, and respect for the body temple. My human experience of addiction delivered me into a sober life which included an understanding that all aspects of evolutionary awakening occur in perfect Divine Order. Perfection is our invisible essence, untouched and unaffected by our Earth School lessons, eventually lead us to cherish and appreciate our perfectly imperfect selves. Perfection is who we are, not what we do. Our souls are whole and complete from the start. Each so-called failure is our invitation to grow spiritually. We are called to make mistakes, fall down and *miss the mark.* However, as we get back up, we grow exponentially. If we are willing to do the work, we will eventually see the perfection and order in all things.

Affirmation: My life is in divine order and it is good. Today I revel in the beauty of my journey and recognize that there are no failures, only victories. And so it is.

A Guide For Success

"I will instruct you and teach you in the way you should go; I will counsel you with my eye upon you."

~Psalms 32:8

The Universe is always inwardly directing our path. The question is, are we open, receptive and listening? Spirit speaks through the intuitive intelligence of the heart and our part is to turn within to catch its guidance, which unconditionally guides us whether we are in a state of confusion or clear mindedness. The point is to turn within under all conditions.

There are times in my life I have caught God's vision but I do not know the next steps to take. During these times I center my awareness and ask two pivotal questions I learned from Michael Bernard Beckwith's book, *The Life Visioning Process*: *"What qualities am I being asked to cultivate to fulfill my life's purpose, and what must I release for the manifestation of the vision?"* I then remain in a state of meditation listening to the still, small voice within.

Sometimes it's a shift in perspective which frees us to launch our life's vision. We must silence the voice of fear, doubt or worry that prevents us from catching the inner guidance. It is time to release the dependency upon old ideas that no longer serve us and resurrect what has always been our true calling in life. It is a time for self-compassion, knowing there is a dancing Spirit at our side, tapping us on the shoulder and reminding us that it is ever-present and guiding us to our highest level of success.

When you feel stuck or not sure what to do, it's time to turn within. Here are some simple but effective questions you can ask yourself. *"Am I expressing my true talents?" "Am I being compassionate with myself?" "Do I see grace in this situation?" "Am I seeing infinite possibilities" "Where am I not seeing God in this situation?" "How can I share more love?" "How can I show more joy?' "How can I share more God?"* True success is when we are truly living out our calling, and share our talents. The only way we can do this is to take a breath, go within and listen for direction.

Affirmation: As I turn within and still my mind, I open my heart to Spirit's vision and guiding steps for its fulfillment. And so it is.

Let Go and Let God Do the God-thing

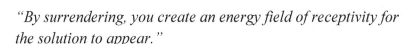

"By surrendering, you create an energy field of receptivity for the solution to appear."

~Wayne W. Dyer

Are you ready to release the illusion of control? When you are willing to surrender your life into a power greater than the little ego you are giving yourself freedom from the need to make things happen. Surrendering to the Higher Self is an activation of the trust, peace, and inherent wisdom within your own soul. It is a state of spiritual maturity that acknowledges you've given up on trying to control God and instead are allowing it to do its *God-thing* in your life.

When Spirit doesn't respond like *SIRI,* answering your every question and satisfying your demands, remind yourself to let go of the false belief that you are fully in control. At the same time, it's a natural human inclination to want to control what will happen in our lives. In fact, the impulsion to do so is implanted in our *Root* chakra whose job description it is to assure our safety and security. Our ancestors experienced this on a daily basis where their physical safety was concerned. We Homo sapiens (a Latin word for "wise man") have evolved and no longer live in caves surrounded by wild animals, yet the urgency to protectively control remains as a mental/emotional aspect of our existence.

When the urge to control is activated in a situation, meet it, acknowledge it and be gentle with yourself. Have a sense of humor about it—pause, breathe, trust, let go, and then with a sense of self-compassion surrender and let Grace do its work. Challenges are an opportunity to grow and to depend on our infinite connection to Spirit. My biggest "Aha" moment: we must learn to trust our divine intuition. There is an overwhelming feeling of peace and calmness when we let God be God! Stop telling the Universe how to show up in our lives. We are co-creating our experience with an omnipotent presence that is always working for our good.

Affirmation: Today, I release and allow God to be God. I surrender to the Divine Power that is always working for my good.

Shaking Up Your Spiritual Plateau

"If you get stuck, draw with a different pen. Change your tools; it may free your thinking."

~Paul Arden

Y ou meditate, pray, spend hours in spiritual study and take classes, however you're still not experiencing the next stage of inner growth you seek. You spend hours reading every book you can but the struggle to stay inspired is real. You are going through what I call the *spiritual plateau*. The truth is, we're in good company as the life stories of the mystics across all spiritual traditions have revealed. Some have even shared the intimate detail times of feeling spiritually dry, stuck, even abandoned by God.

My own interpretation of this sense of spiritual *stuck-ness* can be compared to those times when the physical body has adapted itself to our training regime and won't transform beyond the plateau. That is when I know it's time to respond to the invitation to shakeup the practice, to break free from the habitual pattern in our spiritual routine. It can be as simple as a shift from our favorite meditation chair, moving to the outdoors, a shift in posture, or joining a new meditation group.

The leap into refreshing and or deepening our practice begins with some introspective questions: *"Where does my soul's journey want to take me next?" "How may I best prepare myself for the next level of my spiritual unfoldment?" "What mindsets and old paradigms must I release to make space for this leap?" "Where am I making excuses to avoid change?"* Be compassionately patient with yourself by not forcing answers. They will come when Spirit knows you are ready to receive them, however, inquiring is the vital first step. Ask the questions, trusting your answers will come through the intuitive intelligence of your own heart. This is the work of a spiritual warrior.

Affirmation: Today, I am a spiritual warrior, embracing the spiritual practices. I shake up the habitual routines of life and I embrace my divine expansion.

Expressing God Through Fitness

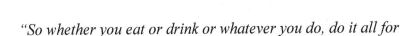

"So whether you eat or drink or whatever you do, do it all for the glory of God."

~1 Corinthians 10:31

"Exercise has a direct brain connection, when you consider what it actually does. What we tend to overlook are the feedback loops that connect the brain to every cell in the body. Therefore when you throw a ball, run on a treadmill, or jog along the shore, billions of cells are 'seeing' the outside world."

~Deepak Chopra

The Mayo clinic has claimed the top 10 excuses for not exercising are: not enough time, exercise is boring, to self-conscious, to tired, to lazy, not athletic, past fitness failure, health club affordability, fear of injury, and family and friend do not support me. In my 30 years of fitness experiences, there is only one deep-rooted block, our inability to see our fitness practice as a spiritual experience.

Here are some practical tips for shifting your fitness into a spiritual practice. See beyond your physical appearance and catch a divine vision of health and fitness for your life. The God presence that lives within you is boundless and as your workout, create a mantra that reminds you of that truth. *"I am strong!"* *"I am healthy!"* *"I am powerful!"* Exercise is a way of expressing God and every time we train we are doing spiritual work. Whether your form of exercise takes place on the dance floor, at the gym, running on a track, jogging with your dog, walking, weight training, aerobics, you get the picture—do it *consciously*.

After a hard vigorous training session, our bodies release hormones called endorphins. I call it the *God Vibration*. The next time you finish your physical practice, take a moment and acknowledge the force running through you. As the Spirit-creates endorphins released throughout your body temple, pause and take a moment to give thanks. Consider creating an affirmation that brings you back to this realization, *"I am vibrant, strong, and healthy because my fitness is a spiritual practice!"*

Affirmation: Right here and right now I declare Spirit is my workout partner as my Godliness flows through me as health, vitality, radiance, peace, compassion and creativity. Amen.

DAY 22

Yoga: A Prayer in Motion

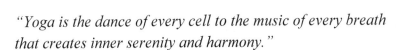

"Yoga is the dance of every cell to the music of every breath that creates inner serenity and harmony."

~**Debasish Mridha**

The Sanskrit word yoga means to bind or bring together, and yoga asana is translated as seat or posture. The practice of Hatha Yoga requires a deep physical, mental and spiritual surrender. When we release the mind's stronghold and surrender to a yoga posture, we are synchronizing body, mind and spirit in union with our spiritual Source. Hatha Yoga prepares us for Raja Yoga, which in the Hindu scripture the *Mahabharata*, is considered to be the royal path to reintegration of one's being—in other words, enlightenment.

Pranayama breathing is the foundation of Hatha Yoga practice and is defined as a refined form of breathing which allows a practitioner to become aware of *prana*, the vital life force circulating throughout one's being, and is known to deliver improved levels of health and wellbeing within and without.

When we are immersed in the depths of Hatha Yoga practice, it is possible to enter a state of mystical prayer wherein thoughts cease and awakened awareness takes over our being. There is no thinking, contemplation, analyzing—there is just simply beingness. This is a result of letting go of all the things outside of ourselves while surrendering to the I AM essence of the Self. The next time you are participating in yoga, consider yourself to be a moving energy of prayer, blessing yourself and radiating out to all beings and our beautiful world.

Affirmation: Today I know myself to be an embodiment of a living, breathing, moving form of prayer that is anchored in conscious union with the Infinite.

Healing Light Within

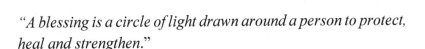

"A blessing is a circle of light drawn around a person to protect, heal and strengthen."

~John O'donohue

Recently, I experienced several injuries due to overtraining my body. Common sense told me to rest, but my ego rudely interrupted saying, "Keep pushing through—don't worry—you'll heal." Although I turned 55 this year and feel more like a young 30, my knees do occasionally reveal their physical age. Because I teach a variety of group fitness classes including yoga, cycling, running and strength exercise, my body doesn't always have sufficient time to rest in between teaching sessions. In my earlier days of fitness training the mantra was, *"no pain, no gain; push through the discomfort,"* concepts, which linger in my subconscious mind and occasionally rise to the level of my conscious mind. To this day I work with compassionately releasing this old paradigm and encourage my clients and students to do the same.

I find the principle of releasing old, worn out paradigms that no longer serve us also applies to the healing of the heart. When we experience heartache, it is an invitation for us to slow down, to compassionately honor our feelings and spiritually work with them. We accomplish this with the full support of the Universe, of Spirit, that constantly whispers its guidance.

In my own life, a regular whisper of guidance says, *"Rest in Me,"* meaning my inner spirit. In order to receive the guidance that is attempting to come through our individual spirit, we must listen in the stillness of the soul. Ultimately, we begin to understand that the power to heal is within our very own *Self.* We, then begin to open ourselves and energize the medicine of Spirit's Healing Light.

Affirmation: I declare my willingness to release old habitual patterns that no longer serve me and energize the Healing Light of my Higher Self.

Intention

"An intention is the reason or motivation for doing what you do. Every action has an intention; it comes from fear or from love."

~Gary Zukav

Did you know goals and intentions are not synonymous? Although in everyday life they are used interchangeably, in truth they are quite different. A goal is an external desired outcome, while an intention is an internal motivation for making a particular choice, for taking a particular action. Goals are projections into the future while intentions for reaching those goals are set in the present moment. Intentions fuel the actions required for reaching our future goals. As Dr. Wayne Dyer writes in *The Power of Intention*, *"Look at intention as a power, not as an action. Imagine that intention is not something you do, but rather a force that exists in the universe as an invisible field of energy."* After reading his book, I was inspired to not only set intensions but to also connect with what he calls the *"faces of intention,"* which he defines as being creativity, kindness, beauty, love, infinite abundance, expansion and receptivity.

From that point on, I became curious and entered a conscious experiment, beginning with creating and embracing my own "faces of intention." *Webster's Universal College Dictionary* defines the word *embrace* as *"to clasp in the arms; to accept willingly: to embrace an idea; to adopt; accept."* This means that every consciously set intention can be an unconditional *"yes"* to embracing our life and the infinite possibilities it contains. Every day we can decide to embrace a "face of intention" and set a tone of openness and receptivity that elevates our Yes Factor. So go ahead, create a list of your own unique *"faces of intention."* Experiment with the power of intention and prove its potency in the laboratory of your own consciousness.

Affirmation: I boldly set my intentions and confidently watch them materialize.

Can You Feel the Love?

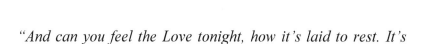

"And can you feel the Love tonight, how it's laid to rest. It's enough to make kings and vagabonds believe the very best."
~Sir Elton John

There is not one moment in our lives that is not infused with Divine Love. Whether or not we are conscious of this truth does not change this fact of life. The Universe offers extraordinary evidence of love. Even so, oftentimes we remain blind to it. There are times we know that Love is all that there is, while at other times we are challenged to find a glimmer of hope. It is important we take the time to acknowledge each of these seemingly contracting experiences have gifts to offer in the form of insights into our being, that we are sufficiently evolved to hold an awareness of love in one hand and our current challenge in the other. Doing so allows us to know that love is always present, even if we don't feel it tangibly in a given moment or specific circumstance in our life.

The heart chakra, or *Anahata* as it's known in Sanskrit, is a shrine of love, compassion, intuition, and is where sacred union is felt with the Divine. When we connect with this chakra in meditation or contemplative prayer, its energy spreads throughout our being. When we connect with another individual, we feel the vibration of this unity in our heart-space. Watching a movie or listening to a song that deeply touches our soul, an upsurge of love floods our being and we may find us spontaneously placing our hand over our heart as if to say, *"I feel you, Love."*

Feeling love moves us to share it with others, to be compassionate givers to those in need, to feel connected in oneness with our global family and offer them prayers of wellbeing, peace, and joy. Love birthed the song *"We Are the World,"* and if you've ever sung it along with others, you can feel the love-energy permeating its lyrics and music. So I ask you, can you feel the Love?

Affirmation: Today, my heart is a storehouse of Divine Love. And when I share it, I am an emissary of God's love.

What Is The Practice?

"Search, no matter what situation you are in. O thirsty one, search for water constantly. Finally, the time will come when you will reach the spring."

~Rumi

When I first began studying yoga, one of the words I heard over and over again was *"practice."* When I landed at the Agape International Spiritual Center, I began to understand the true meaning of the word, which is a staple of its universal teachings. Spiritual practice is a commitment to a daily practice of meditation, affirmative prayer, spiritual study, compassionate service, and generosity of heart for the purpose of expanding one's consciousness and awareness of being one with God and all existence. In India, this would be considered a form of Bhakti Yoga, devotion to the Divine, a path home to our natural state of bliss.

Sometimes we find ourselves sidetracked from our spiritual practice, which even very advanced practitioners experience. We may find that we have become distracted, by seeking the false gods of fame, fortune, or addictions such as drugs, alcohol, work, shopping, sex, food, exercise. We can also be distracted by innocent events like being over-tired or anxiety over the challenges in politics or the lives of our loved ones. Even our practice can become a hiding place for bypassing the inner work we have to do. The good news is when we are honest with ourselves and our spiritual practice is authentic, it wakes and shakes us back to heart's commitment to our inner evolutionary progress.

What I have found supportive of my spiritual growth is to devote 30 days to evolving my practice, even if it means I meditate only 10 minutes a day or read a spiritual teaching for 20 minutes. Don't delay; today is a great day to begin!

Affirmation: As I step into the realization that my entire life is a spiritual practice, I commit to living it with love, gratitude, generosity, creativity, and surrender to the Spirit's vision for my life.

DAY 27

The Source of All Supply

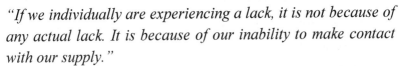

"If we individually are experiencing a lack, it is not because of any actual lack. It is because of our inability to make contact with our supply."

~Joel S. Goldsmith

It was ten years ago when I read my first book about the universal law of supply—Joel Goldsmith's classic, *Invisible Supply*, which is just as fresh in my mind today as it was then. His words, which are quoted above, make it abundantly clear it is our conscious connection to our *Higher Power* that maintains an inner sense of worthiness to receive the constant flow of supply it sends in our direction. When I find myself feeling separate from Source—Spirit itself—it's not only my financial life structure that is affected, but also my overall life is challenged. This feeling of separation, I realized, is rooted in an unwillingness to compassionately forgive myself for however I feel I have transgressed. Stuck in a sense of shame and blame, I meditate and pray less, focus on past experiences of lack, and get stuck. That is, until I shake awake into the reality that I can never be separated from my Source, and that indeed I am deeply blessed because all of my needs are met. It is of supreme benefit to give ourselves the same self-compassion and forgiveness we extend to others, because this is what gets us out of whatever we're stuck in and reconnects to the Reality of our being.

During times when the inner critic won't release its hold, I recall these lyrics from a song we sing at Agape, *Genesis**: *"Stand still and be your own salvation,"* which synchronizes with these words by Goldsmith: *"The Kingdom of God is within you,"* revealing clearly why we are empowered to be our own redemption. And why, when we attune ourselves to our Source of supply miracles happen: we have reclaimed our Divine Inheritance as beings who are individualized expressions of Spirit itself.

Affirmation: Today, my heart is wide-open and I gratefully receive the abundance of gifts! Blessings flow into my life directly from my Higher Power.

*Lyrics by Rickie Byars and Michael Bernard Beckwith.

DAY 28

Dark Night of the Soul

"While the Dark Night of the Soul is a process of death, the Spiritual Awakening Process is the rebirth."

~Mateo Sol

If we are honest, we will admit—if only to ourselves—that at one time or another we have experienced a dark night of the soul. It was the 16th century Spanish mystic and poet, St. John of the Cross, who coined the term "dark night of the soul," which he describes as "a crushing desolation where the soul learns to love again." In my own life there were two experiences of the dark that left me feeling God had forsaken me, both of which occurred right before I was determined to get sober. My desperate prayers seemed to land on deaf ears. No relief or comfort was extended to me in spite of all my efforts. I lashed out, blaming God for abandoning me. These feelings continued into the early months of my sobriety, when I came into the realization that by embracing the dark night one receives the profound gifts, which are hidden within it.

We can also experience what Agape minister Rev. Coco Stewart describes as a "mini-dark night," by which she means a dark night of the senses wherein we temporarily loose sight of the truth of our unbroken connection to God, when our spiritual practices feel as though they are sterile and dry. Whether it's a mini-dark night of the senses or a full-blown dark night of the soul, these challenges come even to those who are solidly devoted to their spiritual practices including highly revered saints, mystics, and spiritual teachers across all spiritual traditions. No one is exempt from the healing that results from walking through the dark night. The good news is that their lives testify to the truth that *"this too shall pass,"* and when it does, we have experienced a transformation in consciousness that always leads back to Love.

During a dark experience, pray until something within your consciousness opens up. Do what connects you to God, allowing Spirit to speak to you through books, teachers, friends and family. This is a time to get still and just be. Whether a dark night of the soul or senses, it will always lead us back to Love. Stay anchored and prayed up Beloved, *"this too shall pass."*

Affirmation: Today, I embrace each dark challenge as an invitation to grow. There is always the glorious morning light after the dark night. And so it is.

DAY 29

I Am Complete and Whole, PERIOD!

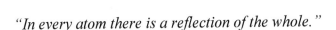

"In every atom there is a reflection of the whole."

~Jay Woodman

In the movie *Jerry Maguire*, Jerry says to Dorothy Boyd, *"You complete me,"* there was an overwhelming sigh in the theater. And from that moment on, that was the tagline that gave the couple the validation to be with each other. Over 20 years after this film's release, I still hear these words of a limited paradigm spoken. The truth is that nothing can complete us, because we are complete from the start.

Understanding we live and move in and as LIFE itself is our spiritual journey. When we believe we become whole because of anything outside of ourselves, we operate in a space of lack and limitation. Self-realization and enlightenment that we are God in the flesh is the only authority we need to live our best life. You are the only one that can measure how much you mean to yourself. Stop looking for a job, a friend, consumerism, material things, or something outside of yourself to tell you that you are good enough. Not only are we good enough, we are enough and this can only be known through our meditation practice. *"Be still and know"* is what the Master Teachers, Jesus, Buddha and many others have invited us to experience. We are the master teachers of our lives. We co-create our existence with God.

Go within, see the wholeness and beauty that is you. Everything you are searching for, you already are. Today, know your complete-self. In your stillness, connect with your Divinity. Our oneness with Source gives us the permission and the validity to live a life that is whole and complete PERIOD! We exist because we are the *I AM*. *"Cogito ergo sum,"* in Latin means, I think therefore I am. Today let's shift that statement; I meditate, therefore I am.

Affirmation: Today, I am the complete and whole expression of the Divine. And so it is, and so I am, and so I will always be.

Teachings from Nature

"Reading about nature is fine, but if a person walks in the woods and listens carefully, he can learn more than what is in books, for they speak of the voice of God."
~George Washington Carver

W est African elder, spiritual teacher and author Dr. Malidoma Patrice Somé teaches we are not only cohabitating with nature, we are nature itself. The greatest way to recognize our oneness in God is in nature. When we are present in the vastness of Mother Earth, we can feel divine vibration radiating throughout our soul.

When was the last time you walked barefoot on the beach and felt the sand sifting between your toes, or looked up into the limitlessness of the night sky and paid homage to the stars? How long has it been since you paused during a walk to hear one of our feathered friends sing the universal song of life? These gifts are freely offered by Mother Nature, and they are yours if you allow yourself to receive them. Listen! Listen deeply, and you will realize She is sharing Her secrets with you. Humble yourself, be teachable, and commune. You might ask the Universe what is seeking to emerge from this moment of divine communion. When the answer comes, record them in your heart and later in a journal so you may refer back to the *"Aha-download."*

Set an intention to be a student of Mother Nature. Remember, when George Washington Carver asked God to show him the secrets of the universe, his attention was drawn to a plant that was considered to be of minimal purpose. Carver went on to discover over 300 uses for the peanut and over 100 sweet potato products. Just imagine what is possible when you open yourself to the Earth's gifts!

Affirmation: Today I dance to the music of Mother Earth and celebrate my oneness with Her beauty, intelligence, generosity, and humility as I attune myself to the secrets of the Universe.

The Choice To Forgive

"A lack of self-forgiveness is a form of self-abuse."
~Michael Bernard Beckwith

"Before you pray, forgive."

~Mary A. Tumpkin

In Brene Brown's book *The Gifts of Imperfection*, she writes that we learn more from our failures than our successes. My life experience has taught me she is 100% right! Welcome to Earth School! Missing the so-called *mark* is a key ingredient for transformation. As our learning process unfolds, it is vital to keep in mind self-love. It is a given in life that we will make mistakes; the point is not to let the ego prevent us from learning from them. We must not continue in a victim consciousness by blaming circumstances outside of ourselves.

When we choose to grow and transform, our process will always include successes and challenges disguised as failures. If we have missed our desired mark, it isn't a failure or a defeat, just an invitation to evolve. It doesn't matter how many times we fall, it only matters that we get back up, dust ourselves off and continue the transformative process.

Cultural, religious and educational conditioning has taught us that the harsh words of the inner critic serve as a motivator for a temporary change, but self-forgiveness, positivity and encouragement is a much more loving energy that paves the way for lasting transformation. So why not make the choice to love yourself through challenges rather than beating yourself up? When we choose self-forgiveness, we choose love, God's unconditional love which includes all of who we are, a God who sees us as whole, perfect, and complete just as we are in any given moment, and who supports us every step of the way.

Affirmation: Today, I compassionately forgive myself; therefore, I am forgiven. I love myself; therefore, I am loved. And so it is that I am able to extend my love and forgiveness to others.

Author's Reflections

*"Your transportation to transformation is your very own Self,
and you are already fully equipped with all that you need for
the journey. Savor every step of the way!"*

~Michael Bernard Beckwith

On July 15, 2018, my spiritual home, the Agape International Spiritual Center, held its last service in a building it had occupied for 20 years and was preparing for its move to the Saban Theatre is Beverly Hills. Its founder, Dr. Michael Bernard Beckwith, delivered his final teaching in a space that was permeated with all the love, joy, wisdom and celebration of the Spirit its congregation and live streamers experienced every Sunday and Wednesday—not to mention all the weddings, christenings, memorial services and student graduations from its classes. On this significant Sunday, I sat next to my best friend, Bill. It was a bittersweet moment as we wrapped our arms around each other and cried, laughed, and reminisced about what we had come to call our *"Agape Moments."* Our memories transported us back to 2008, when the Agape International Choir sang with John Legend and Will-I-am, and when in January 2009 it traveled to Washington, D.C. to sing at the inauguration of President Barack Obama. All this as we simultaneously looked forward to what awaited the Beloved Community in our new location.

Dr. Beckwith spoke on the *Four Domains of Living,* which are: *Survival, Adaptation, Transformation and Desolation.* Most people live in the survival and adaptation domain, worrying about how to make it day-to-day, adapting life's circumstances making choices for the pure purpose to survive. Some people become very successful in these two domains and never evolve. We learn to adapt through coping, behavior and defense mechanisms like drugs, sex, over shopping and strategizing. This behavior keeps people in this old paradigm of materialism, consumerism, and becoming a celebrity instead of being a useful presence on the planet.

The transformation and desolation domains are where the pioneers and innovators are bringing a new paradigm to our existence. This is where the urban shamans, artists, healers, meditators and visionaries' practice, allowing divine ideas to emerge through their souls. Transformation ushers in the next expression of whom we are as a species, but the desolation domain releases everything that longer serves the vision. As Michael spoke, I realized this is my evolution, a journey from addition to minster. When I landed at the Agape International Spiritual Center, I was in survival and adaption mode *struggling just to make it through another day* as the song as my favorite song "I Release," speaks. Today, because of my spiritual practices, I live in the transformation and desolation domain. Through art, yoga, and ministry, I live with a purpose and my life has meaning.

When we choose to transform our lives, there are always stages in our transformation. Stage one, we see the need for a change, but change is always external, temporary and unfulfilling. Stage two, we desire a deeper transformation and so begin our quest for freedom. This requires the spiritual practices of prayer, meditation and sacred study. Stage three is the evolution. When we commit to expanding our consciousness, there is always a physical, mental and spiritual evolution that cannot be stopped. We evolve to a higher state of existence.

This *Little Book for Big Transformation* is a testament to my journey. My wish for you *Beloved* is that you be willing to do the spiritual work so you may have your personal evolution. The first thing I learned on this spiritual path; there is no destination only the journey, any we learn how to fall in love with the journey. The following five principles and practices help me daily on this passageway of transformation. I offer them with a prayer that they may be of service to you by enriching your heart and energizing your desire to follow the unique path of your own soul's calling.

1. **CARES: Connection, Action, Remember, Empowerment, Self-love.** Connection to our Higher Self is the key to transforming our lives. Every intention requires action to achieve our desired goals. Transformation occurs through the remembrance of our true nature. Every moment of our evolutionary process reveals we are already empowered for enlightened

living. Self-love comes from the nourishment of our own heart, which keeps us steadfast on the path to awakening, encouraging us every step of the way.

2. **The 3 Bs: Believe, Breathe, Be.** Believe all challenges *came to pass*, not to stay. Believe there is something seeking to emerge from the situation for the highest good of your life. Breathe: it is the breath that allows us to reconnect with life. Breathe because the Universe is always working for our highest good. Be - Just Be. Every challenge is designed for us to grow, but we must be in it, so we may grow through it. Instead of wishing away our challenges, embrace it. Be authentic! Be kind to yourself and others. Just BE!!

3. **Flow = Faith, Love, Open, Willingness.** Have faith that you are in the place, having the right experience at the right time. Love yourself through every stage of the transformational journey. Stay open for new insights and *Aha moments* to come through as you. If we are willing to grow, transformation will happen. Be willing to do the work; a shift is inevitable. Sometimes we only need to be willing, to be willing.

4. **5 D's of Transformation: Drive, Dedication, Determination, Discipline and Direction.** Always remember what is driving you. Stay connected to your intentions. Stay dedicated to your transformation one breath at a time. Determination is a mindset to stay with

something. You must go through it, so that you may growth from it. Discipline is a practice that is done over and over again, until we find our bliss. Then the practice becomes a blissipline. Direction will come when we humble ourselves and allow the universe to teach up. When the student is ready the teach will appear.

5. **It is done as you believe.** The word mantra in Sanskrit means "tool for the mind." The greatest mantra we have is I AM. How we use the I am mantra is key. We can use it with a high vibrational frequency or as a low undesirable statement of truth. The Universe always responds with a yes. When we say, "I am tired, I am sick, I am poor, I am unlovable" that is our statement of truth and it is followed by a universal yes. But when use the I am mantra followed by a positive declaration; we unleash the power for transformation. "I am powerful, I am blessed, I am abundant," helps to shift your thinking.

I want to compete this experience by expressing my gratitude and thanksgiving for you as a fellow traveler on your transformational path. Remember, you are on purpose with a purpose. May you answer the call of your soul and find the joy, tranquility, and contentment that is your Divine Inheritance.

Peace and Blessings,

SKIP

71

About the Author

Skip Jennings is an Agape Licensed Spiritual Practitioner a graduate of The Michael Bernard Beckwith School of Ministry in the New Thought-Ageless Wisdom tradition of spirituality. He is the author of *The Lotus Kitchen* and *Spirit Explosion*. As a motivational speaker, transformational coach, and founder of the Mind, Body, Spirit Solution LLC, Skip travels the world teaching his empowerment method called CARES, an acronym for Connection, Action, Remembering, Empowerment, and Self-love. You can learn more about Skip's coaching and expertise at SkipJennings.com, YouTube, Instagram, Facebook, Twitter and many other online blogs. With 30 years of experience, over fifteen qualifications in wellness, health, fitness and nutrition, Skip continues to help transform the planet one life at a time.

CPSIA information can be obtained
at www.ICGtesting.com
Printed in the USA
LVHW080730240821
695886LV00007B/885